Value Based Marketing

How People Decide To Buy

LON SAFKO

Copyright © by Lon S. Safko

All rights reserved. No part of this book may be used or reproduced by any means, graphic, electronic, or mechanical, including photocopying, recording, taping or by any information storage retrieval system without the written permission of the publisher except in the case of brief quotations embodied in critical articles and reviews.

Printed in the United States of America

This book was created using 100% recycled electrons

No animals were harmed in the making of this book

This book is dolphin safe

The Value Equation
How People Decide To Buy

In marketing, one brand is always trying to outwit, out advertise, and out spend its competitors, often costing millions of dollars to build their brand equity or brand value. It's because, the better we recognize a brand, the better we relate to that brand, the higher the value that brand has in our minds and the safer we feel purchasing that brand. The higher the brand value in the minds of the consumers, the more those prospects will purchase that brand, generating greater revenues for that brand company.

Brand value is in the mind of the customer. It's no more than a perception. Change the perception and you change the perceived brand value.

The smallest perceived difference in Value can seal the deal!

It's about this psychological sense of balance,
And, it's on going…

The value of a brand or the value of a purchase looks like this. Whether you realize you are making these calculations consciously or subconsciously, you are making many calculations before you make a purchase. This holds true for your last new car and your last pack of gum. This process is independent of the cost of the product. Only the buying cycle changes.

Think about the last time you purchased something from a convenient store. You know that you could have bought that quart of milk, six pack of beer, or loaf of bread much cheaper at the grocery store, right?

You weighed out the grocery store experience first. You knew you had to park 100 feet from the building, walk another 100 feet to the back of the store for that quart of milk, then 100 feet back to the register, wait in line while "coupon lady" goes through 200 coupons on her two grocery carts of cat litter and TV dinners, then walk the 100 feet back to your car.

Or, you could pull up to a convenient store, 8 feet from the door, walk only 20 feet to the milk and get through the cashier line in under 3 minutes (average wait time in convenient store check out lines across the U.S.).

We are purchasing the convenience. When you add the additional cost of the product at a convenient store, then subtract all of the negative we encounter at the grocery store, often, the value equation determines that it a higher value to pay more to get more convenience.

Question: Have you ever paid more for something just to get it sooner? I rest my case.

The Conversion Equation

Everyone is looking for a secret equation, secret formula, the secret sauce, the Holy Grail in marketing, especially social media and digital marketing.

Hint: There is NO secret formula! There are some rules; however. There are a few formulas you can follow to increase your probability of success.

Sales and conversion are psychological concepts. The question of "how can I retain, convert, and ultimately generate sales from a prospect or customer is a soft science. Psychology is a soft science. Psychology doesn't work the same way as physics or engineering, where 1 + 1 always equals 2 or the diameter of a circle is always the diameter times Pi.

Psychology uses terms like probability and graphs like a bell curve to determine the probable outcome of a given set of psychological data. Retention, conversion, and sales are all part of this soft science probability.

$$P(0) = \frac{2!}{0!(2-0)!}(.5^0)(1-.5)^{2-0} = \frac{2}{2}(1)(.25) = 0.25$$

$$P(1) = \frac{2!}{1!(2-1)!}(.5^1)(1-.5)^{2-1} = \frac{2}{1}(.5)(.5) = 0.50$$

$$P(2) = \frac{2!}{2!(2-2)!}(.5^2)(1-.5)^{2-2} = \frac{2}{2}(.25)(1) = 0.25$$

And,

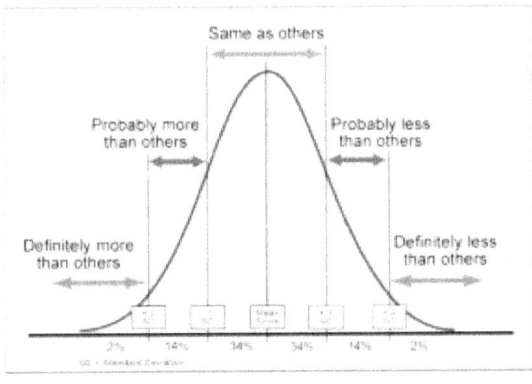

Teaching these concepts to executives from around the globe has forced me to become more introspective and has intrigued me to find a more definitive answer to the conversion equation.

Defining "conversion" as only a soft science probability equation, I felt was a cop-op. So I decided to take a more serious look at what I did know about the subject and what could be argued as mathematics or probability.

The difficulty of developing an equation for conversion is that while a specific set of data, examples, and numbers may be true for this company, the outcome of the equation for a different company can vary wildly. And using the exact same equation and data within the same company for a different product, has a different outcome entirely. And... often using the same equation and same data that has proven successful in the past for the same company and the same product has different results when executed a second or third time.

We've even seen results where only a very slight change in the data can generate disastrous outcomes such as the Starbuck's Christmas Coffee Cup "Controversy" or the New Coke / Classic Coke disaster.

Starbuck's 2014 Christmas Cups - A Big Hit

Starbuck's 2015 Christmas Cups - A PR Nightmare

New Coke versus Classic Coke of 1985

The problem with determining an exact equation for "what works" is that we are dealing with human perception. What makes someone buy your product versus a competitor's product or why someone opens your April email, but opts out of your May email is all about perception. And, as we all know this is a huge variable.

Everyone has different perceptions based on values, morays, education, culture, religious beliefs, economic status, sex, age, and how they view the world on any particular day.

After studying what I did know to be true about sales, conversion, value, frequency, and revenue did lead me to a secret formula. Here is is:

$$R = \frac{v}{f} \Rightarrow C, \text{ whereas } C \Rightarrow S$$

Whereas R equals Retention, v = Value, f = Frequency and C = Conversion or Sales.
When I teach advanced digital marketing, I simplify the process by saying, social media gives you a platform which allows you to interact and gain access to a huge number of prospects, e.g.: Facebook with 1,550,000,000 members, LinkedIn at 396,000 members, or Twitter with 307,000,000 members. And that, this access gives us as marketers the opportunity to build relationships with prospects, because relationships lead to trust, trust leads to sales.

There are two primary truths here; one is that you don't buy a product or service from a company or salesperson you don't trust and the other is, not everyone is ready to purchase your product or service, today. As a result, we must keep our name, logo, and brand in front of our prospects so when they are ready to purchase, they think of you first. This is the purest definition of mass marketing. It's what drives McDonal's to Mercedes.

Just because you saw a Mercedes automobile commercial last night nestled in between your reality shows or sit-coms on TV, didn't mean that you suddenly realized that you need a new car, perhaps a Mercedes, and ran out and bought one.

Large brands know the investment necessary to stay in front of their prospects until they are ready to purchase. This is called the buying cycle. Another truth is, the buying cycle is different for every product and is usually based on the purchase price; the less expensive the product, the shorter the cycle and conversely, the more expensive the product the longer the cycle.

This is why a new car buying cycle is usually around three years and a pack of gum is an "impulse" instant purchase.

All of this leads to another critical question, what is the correct "frequency" (f) of contact should I have with my prospects to maximize conversion. The short answer is, it depends on two variable, the form of communication and the value of the content to the recipient. Are are several examples.

When I communicate with my prospects using the social platform Twitter, I send out three tweets every day, Monday through Friday. This means that I contact my prospects 15 times, every week. What if... I sent you 15 emails every week, week in and week out. What would you do? Contact Interpol and have me arrested? Contact a mob boss and have me killed? Exactly!

Using the email platform, frequency is governed by the technology and what we perceive as appropriate. In the case of email, if I contacted you, maybe once or twice a month, you would fine that acceptable. However, on Twitter, it is perfectly acceptable for me to contact you 15 times a week or 60 times every month. That's the power behind Twitter. It is acceptable for me to put my name and my brand in front of you 60 times each month! But, these truths also lead to another truth, the value of the content (v).

When teaching, I use the email scenario, where a few years back, I purchased a new Macintosh computer. After the sale, I got an email from the company I bought my Mac from every week. Every week. I don't know about you, but I don't buy a new Mac every week, or every month, or even every year. As a result of what I thought as incisive spam, I unsubscribed.

At about the same time, I bought a new fish tank for my office. After the sale, I began receiving emails from the manufacturer, one each week. There was a big difference with this company. Their emails said "Hey, this is the first week of the month. Did you remember to change the water in your tank?". The next email was, Hello Lon, this is the second week of the month, have you changed your carbon filter lately?". Every week's email reminded me that there was a critical task that if I didn't do, would result in the death of my fish and loss of my investment.

With the amount of international travel that I do, a reminder to clean the filter, test the PH, or change the water is something I could have easily forgotten with dire consequences. The value of these communications were very important to me so the acceptable level of frequency can be significantly higher.

While the frequency of the Mac store and the fish tank manufacturer was identical, the value of the content varied greatly. One had little value so I fired that company as a provider, while the other had high value to me, so I allowed them to essentially market to me every week.

Another short example is about a year ago, my wife signed up for a Starbuck's card. She would load it with $25 increments and reload it again when it emptied. Starbuck's would send her a notice when she purchased enough product to earn her a free cup of coffee or when it was her birthday and there was another free coffee waiting for her. She liked that.

Then, over the past year the frequency of the emails grew to an email, every day. These emails told her that she could participate in earning points for sales or something. This morning she decided to "unsubscribe" from Starbucks email blast and officially switch over to Circle K coffee. The frequency versus value equation forced to to evaluate the inconvenience of daily emails from Starbuck's with content that had no value to her.

If it were a daily email with a code for a free cup of coffee every day, She would have welcomed their emails. By overstepping their frequency while at the same time offer little or no value, Starbuck's not only lost her from their ability to market products to her, they actually lost her as a valued repeat customer.

Whether you have been aware of this correlation or not, you must agree that it is human nature to perceive communications this way.

Distilling all of the above conversation down to a secret formula, you get this:

$$R = \frac{v}{f} \Rightarrow C, \text{ whereas } C \Rightarrow S$$

Whereas R equals Retention, v = Value, f = Frequency and C = Conversion or Sales.
If you want to keep your brand in front of your prospects during their entire buying cycle so when they are ready to purchase, they purchase from you, you have to communicate with them frequently.

The frequency depends on the platform or tool you use for communication.
The frequency is more dependent on the value of the content. So…

Given a particular communications tool, the greater the value of content, the great the frequency and the higher probability you will convert that prospect from a prospect into a customer, which will leads to an increase in sales.

COMPARATIVE VALUE

Here's another example of how Innovation works on a more complex problem:

I developed this concept of Comparative Value Analysis when I was working on a classified project for the United States Department of Energy, Westinghouse Electric, on the Hanford Nuclear Reservation in Richland Washington.

I was the project manager, responsible for the development of an artificial inelegance, quality assurance, trend analysis system for analyzing the handling of plutonium, tritium, and uranium for reactors and national defense both new production and nuclear waste.

It became apparent that every situation has a different number of important variables and different level of importance for each item. Innovative Thinking determines that in order to analyze reports, public perception, products, sales techniques, marketing programs, and nuclear waste, these items must be weighted. This became the basis for this system analysis.

I used Comparative Value Analysis in a practical application again in 1994, while consulting for Honda in Denver, who said their salespeople had difficulty in explaining the value of all of the options they offered against the options of their competitor. They all had different options, different pricing, and different options came standard.

They wanted to allow the customer to be able to understand that their particular model with it's particular options was a better value than their competitors model similarly equipped.

After thinking about it for a long while, I applied the 5-W's of Innovative Thinking process to the problem. Here's what happened:

> **1. What:** Determine if there is a problem, then identify the problem.
> Is there a problem? Yes, It's too difficult for customers to understand the value of the combinations and permutations of model automobiles and options.
>
>> **a.** Can I make it easier to understand. More quantitative and less qualitative.
>
> **2. Who:** Who is affected by this problem? There are two groups affected. Both have trouble comprehending and comparing value between models and options.
>
>> **a.** The customer doesn't comprehend which

leads to a difficult buying decision.

b. The salesman loses the sale 50% of the time due to a wrong customer decision.

3. Why: Why does it happen?

a. There are too many desirable options, all with different prices, all added to a different base sticker amount, all with different perceptions of value for each option, all from different manufacturers. The customer is unable to compare, models, options, values, and prices, simultaneously.

4. When: When does this type of analysis become important?

a. This tool becomes important at the point of sale, the most critical time.

5. Where: Where are other solutions that might either help, cause it not to happen or do I have to create it myself?

a. There are many different types of grading systems to try to convert qualitative data and make it more quantifiable. The A's, B's, and C's of school convert "Plays well with others" to a "B", which can be translated to an 80 to 90%.

b. And there are other grading systems, pigeon holing, and estimating that helps make these translations.

5. How: How do I fix it?
Follow step 5 in the 5-W's of Innovative Thinking and identify any possible solutions, any similar solutions, or create it yourself.

a. Identify a possible solutions for this particular problem.

b. There are no known systems for doing this, specifically.

c. Knowing B from above, I realize that I have

to create the solution. What is known is that if I create a grading system that applies a value to each option and compares it to price and perceived value, I could create a formula that will be a "plug-and-play" evaluation.

Now we're down to the final solution: How do I create a solution that satisfies the above criteria?

Here's the thought process:
As with most qualitative decision-making processes, it's difficult to analyze from a quantitative perspective. In order to quantitatively compare the "value" of a product, we must convert qualitative observations to empirical data. Let's perform the following on two or more products similar in nature and arrive at a numeric comparison, which I call "Comparative Value Index" or (CVI).

Let's make the following assumption:

Purchases are made based on perceptions of Value; Value is a function of Quality, Functionality, Service, and Price; and Product Value is a comparison of the

CVI between two competing products.

Then the following is true:

$$V = \frac{Q * F * S}{P}$$

V = Value or the Comparative Value Index;

Q = Quality of workmanship and reliability, rated between 0 - 9;

F = The importance of a product's Functionality. List all functions and rate them between 0 - 9, then add them together;

S = The level of Service and support including response time, level of knowledge, willingness to 'stand behind the product' with complimentary / warranty, or reduced pricing on product or servicing of the product, and;
P = Product Price.

To make this example easier to work through, let's take a simple example, the purchase of a wrench. Let's analyze an SAE wrench against a Craftsman wrench;

Q = Snap-On brand would be the best at a 9, while Craftsman at an 8, and SAE at a 7;

F = They all are functionally equal and work as well to tighten or loosen a nut. Let's give them all a 9;

S = SAE, is up to the discretion of the clerk or store owner at a 6, Craftsman is an unconditional warranty at a 9;

P = SAE $2.99 and Craftsman at $3.99.

SAE Wrench **Craftsman Wrench**

$$V = \frac{7 * 9 * 6}{2.99} = 126 \qquad V = \frac{8 * 9 * 9}{3.99} = 162$$

The Craftsman Wrench weighs in at a 162 while the SAE weighs in at a 126. Even though the Craftsman is more expensive, the total 'value' of the Craftsman wrench is greater. Buy the Craftsman wrench!

Summary of Innovative Solution:

Does this formula meet all of the requirements of an Innovative Solution?

Does it work? - YES!

Is it cost effective? - YES! (it's free)

Is it a simple solution? --YES! (plug-and-play)

Is it timely? - YES! (available right now)

Is it moral and legal? - YES! (sure is)

Is it easy to implement? - YES! (just start using it)

Then, we found an Innovative Solution!

For more information about the author, please visit www.LonSafko.com